Creepy, Crawly

AND FASCINATING INSECTS OF NORTH FLORIDA

Written by Tomi Saga

Illustrated by Mackenzie Ott

For my grandchildren
and nature explorers everywhere. -TS

Copyright © 2025 by Tomi Saga

Published by Tomi Elsagga. For permission requests or ordering information, please contact: catintheattic789@gmail.com

Illustrations by Mackenzie Ott.

All rights reserved. No part of this publication may be reproduced, distributed, or transmitted in any form or by any means, including photocopying, recording, or other electronic or mechanical methods without prior written permission from the publisher, except in the case of brief quotations embodied in critical reviews and certain other noncommercial uses permitted by copyright law.

ISBN 978-1-7375548-9-9 (hardcover) • ISBN 979-8-9901490-0-7 (paperback)
ISBN 979-8-9901490-1-4 (ebook)

Book design by the Virtual Paintbrush. Text was set in Goudy Bookletter 1911.

Have bugs been around for a long time? Yes, they have! Fossils of insects were found on rocks dating back more than 400 million years ago. That's before dinosaurs and way before mankind! And some of their distant cousins are living and crawling in our North Florida forests, fields, and even our back yards right now! Wow! In science, insects are animals called Arthropods. There are millions of insects in the world of all sizes, shapes, and colors. Some move fast, and some move slowly. Some are picky eaters, and some aren't. Some do funny things, and some are not funny. They're venomous, and they sting, sometimes sending you to the hospital! Some are tricky. Some are weird and creepy. Some are pretty, and some are pretty scary! They are creepy, crawly, and very fascinating.

A long time ago in ancient Greece (over 3,000 years ago) Entomen was the word for insect and Logy meant the study of something. So, both words together are Entomology, which means the study of insects. A person who studies insects is called an Entomologist.

Then, about two thousand years ago, in Latin (an old language from Italy) insects got their present name because they look like they are (cut-into-sections). Insects are very small animals that have three sections: a Head for eating, a Thorax for moving with legs and wings, and an Abdomen for laying eggs, pooping, and stinging. (Did you know only female insects sting?)

Now, let's take a peek and read about some very interesting bugs that live in beautiful North Florida.

Rhinoceros Beetle

THIS IS A very big and mighty beetle. The male rhinoceros beetle can grow four inches long and has a horn on its head, just like a rhinoceros! With swagger, these big beetles use their strength and horns to fight other males. It is said that a male beetle can lift to 100 times its weight. That would be like a man lifting two full-grown elephants. Incredible!

When two male rhinoceros beetles meet face to face, it looks like a beetle wrestling match. They don't kill each other, but they flip and toss each other about with their horns. The loser gets tossed off the tree branch, falling to the ground. The winner gets a lovely lady rhinoceros beetle for his mate!

Fun Facts

- Do bugs have blood? Yes, they do! Their kind of blood is not red like ours. It's a clear fluid in their body called hemolymph.
- Female rhinoceros beetles don't have horns.
- Rhinoceros beetles like to eat leaves, fruits, and flower nectar, and they don't bother people.

Oowwchh!!! It's a painful hot mess if you step on a fire ant nest! These fierce little ants are a force of nature. No matter how nice you are, there's no way you can be friends with them. Yet these little creatures show an enormous and extraordinary level of care and cooperation for fellow ants within their colony.

Way below the ground, they have a united, organized, hard-working civilization with vast tunnels and chambers for specific uses. There are chambers for food stock, for trash, for a nursery, and a mother's chamber where the queen lays her eggs. There's even a tomb chamber, where dead ants are carried and buried. Different ants carry out different jobs.

If you step on their mound, they'll be mad as frogs and instantly come out to attack. Most of them are females, and they're fiercely protecting the queen and her eggs. A single ant can keep re-stinging you three or more times! Many people have been hospitalized by fire ants' stings.

Stay away from fire ants and run to get help from a grownup if you or a family member step on a fire ant nest. You could help them get medical treatment if needed.

Fun Facts

- A fire ant has an astounding sense of smell for food. It can detect food from a distance of 300 feet.
- An ant cannot die of falling from any height! (The wind resistance makes them unable to die from falling.)
- Dead ants release a pheromone chemical that is to alarm the colony. As soon as other ants detect this smell, they go out to collect the dead body. Then they carry it away to their tomb chamber to be buried.
- A queen ant can lay up to 1,500 eggs per day! (No wonder she sleeps a lot!)
- A single ant nest can house between 100,000 to 500,000 ants!
- A queen ant can live up to seven years or more.
- A fire ant mound can go 20 feet deep below the ground or more and extend out eight feet in all directions.
- A queen ant can sleep about nine hours a day. Worker ants take lots of power naps. (No wonder they're so swift to sting!)

Yes, stink bugs do make a stink! But only if they sense danger. This bug sprays a strong odor in the air to defend itself from enemies. Kinda like a bug fart!

Stink bugs don't have mouths to chew or bite, so how do they eat? Green stink bugs have special mouth parts that suck the sap and juice of plants. It's sort of their own smoothie-making machine!

Stink bugs chat with their buddies and find a mate by using vibrations. They move their bodies in a way that vibrates the plants. That's how they talk to each other. It's their very own silent secret language.

Fun Facts

- Stink bugs' stink smells like citronella and bug spray.
- Stink bugs don't bother people.
- Stink bugs come in different colors.

Cicada
(Sih-KAY-duh)

CICADA MEANS *tree cricket* in Latin, (an Old Italian language). These red-eyed, alien-looking bugs do a lot of chatter. They're the loudest insects in the world! In summer in North Florida, you can hear these big, loud tree crickets high up in the trees. The male cicadas are singing and serenading to find a female mate. They're kind of scary looking, but I'm sure the lady cicadas think they're handsome! When they find their mate, the female digs holes in branches to lay her eggs. Then, when they hatch, the baby cicadas (called NYMPHS) crawl down the tree, burrow in the ground, and there they stay, underground for a year, eating tree sap and growing. In some states, the cicadas stay in the ground for 10, 13, or even 17 years! Then, they come out as adults, sing to find a mate, and the cicada's circle of life starts all over again.

Fun Facts

- Fun fact: When cicadas MOLT (shed their skin), they leave their empty body shells attached to tree trunks.
- Fun fact: Cicadas have five eyes all together! Two bigger red eyes on the side of their head and three smaller eyes in a triangle shape in the front of their head.

Eastern Eyed Click Beetle

THIS BEETLE IS a little rascal. It pretends and plays tricks. When threatened by a predator, it can click and flip on its back, not even move, and pretend it's dead! It has a spine-like structure between its body segments which allows it to do that. And then, when the predator is gone, it clicks, flips back on its legs and crawls away!

It also has two black circles near its head that look just like big black eyes. But they're not eyes! It is thought that these big fake eyes are meant to scare away its enemies.

Fun (& Spooky!) Facts

- Click beetles don't bother people. They eat pollen and flower nectar.
- In the old days in Wales (a country inside the United Kingdom), the Old Welsh word *Bwg* (pronounced *boog*) was used to describe a ghost or goblin. They believed a ghostly boogeyman bit their children at night when they slept because there were red marks on their body when they woke up. They didn't know it was not goblins. The marks were from teeny-tiny bedbugs sucking their blood at night! That's where the words bug (*bwg*) and boogeyman come from!
- Did you ever wonder where the saying *"sleep tight, don't let the bedbugs bite"* comes from? It started in the 16th century, about 500 years ago. In those days, wooden bed frames had ropes to support mattresses. When the ropes got loose and saggy they needed to be tightened. Mattresses in those days were stuffed with straw and feathers. Bedbugs liked to live in the straw and feathers. So that's where, *"sleep tight (tight ropes), don't let the bedbugs bite"* comes from!

Like all other insects, a butterfly has three sections: a head, a thorax, and an abdomen. Except they also have beautiful delicate wings to fly.

Around the world, there are legends about butterflies. The ancient Aztecs believed the migrating monarch butterflies carried the souls of their ancestors, who return to Earth for their annual visit. In modern-day Mexico each November, the festival of *Dia de los Muertos* (the Day of the Dead), continues this tradition. American Indian legends say that if anyone wants a wish to come true, they must first gently catch a butterfly, whisper that wish to it, and let it go.

In North Florida, we have lots of orange-and-black butterflies that look like monarchs but are named gulf fritillaries.

The female will only lay her itty-bitty eggs on the passion vine (their host plant), which grows in North Florida. When the eggs hatch, teeny-tiny caterpillars emerge and begin nibbling the passion vine leaves till they get bigger and fatter.

Soon it's time for the caterpillar to make a hard case called a chrysalis. And then, in a swirl of mystery, it PUPATES (rests and transforms) for 11 to 21 days. When the time is just right, it becomes an adult and emerges as a butterfly.

This is called METAMORPHOSIS, an ancient Greek word for "changing shape." The butterfly will fly, look for flower nectar, and find a mate. Then the female will lay her eggs on the passion vine leaves, and the gulf fritillary's cycle of life will start all over again.

Fun Facts

- Long ago in Germany, dairy farmers believed witches turned themselves into butterflies to steal or lick their butter. "Butterlicker" is a word for butterfly in German. It's where we got the name *butterfly* today.
- Butterflies were sacred to the ancient Aztecs. They believed butterflies were in charge of taking the beloved souls of warriors who died in battle and women who died giving birth, to their resting place.

IF YOU COME across a green leaf walking, you've found a katydid! This pretty, bright-green bug cleverly disguises itself as a leaf for CAMOUFLAGE from predators. Their wings look like two leaves that lay flat on each side of their body. They rub their front wings together to make cricket sounds at night. And if you listen closely, people say it sounds like "katydid" and "katy didn't." The katydid has kind of a cute face. A baby katydid is called a NYMPH, and it is really cute looking.

Fun Facts

- They say the katydid night sounds are like crickets with a repeated rhythm sounding like katydid and katy didn't. But you can make up what you think it sounds like. I think it sounds like Cha-cha-cha, Cha-cha-cha! Let's dance!
- Katydids don't bother people.

Tiger Beetle

THIS BEETLE DOESN'T look like a tiger but gets its name from how fast it moves and how fierce it is to its prey. This beetle is so extremely fast, it's said that the tiger beetle moves at 171 times its body length per second! So, that means in one second, it can move a distance of 171 times its own length. That's lightning fast! Its prey can barely notice it coming, much less escape! Then the tiger beetle grabs its victim with its MANDIBLES (claw-like jaws on the sides of its mouth), much like a tiny ferocious tiger.

Fun Facts

- To explain how blazing fast the tiger beetle is, a cheetah (the fastest mammal on Earth) can run at 16 body lengths per second, and a tiger beetle can run at 171 body lengths per second!
- In fact, the tiger beetle goes so fast that they go blind for a few seconds, because their brains can't keep up with their speed. They must stop running so their brains can catch up to see again!
- Tiger beetles are considered a beneficial insect. They eat other beetles, flies, caterpillars, spiders, ants, and more. They don't bother people.

Lubber Grasshopper

THE WORD *LUBBER* is an Old English word for "lazy" because these grasshoppers are so slow. They are big, colorful, hungry, and as slow as a herd of turtles. The lubber grasshopper takes its time slowly gobbling up favorite garden plants, while driving gardeners bananas.

If you bother one, it may get mad, spread its colorful wings, and hiss at you. Or even spit a brown chemical a distance of six inches toward you. Watch out, yuck!

Fun (& Yukky!) Facts

- The grasshopper's BROWN SPIT is commonly called tobacco juice. It's made from digested plants and stomach enzymes.
- Lubber grasshoppers have ears on their bellies.

Dogbane Beetle

THIS VERY PICKY and beautiful colored beetle got its name from the only plant it eats: the dogbane plant, which grows in North Florida. The dogbane beetle has bright, shiny colors of green, gold, and blue that are IRIDESCENT, which means they shimmer in the sun. But their pretty color is a warning sign because the sap from the dogbane plant is poisonous, and it also makes them poisonous if eaten by their predators.

Fun Facts

- The dogbane plant is a member of the milkweed family of plants because they have a milky sap that's poisonous to people and animals.
- Thousands of years ago, Native Americans used dried dogbane stems to make a good rope. And we still make rope from it today. When it's dried, there's no more poisonous sap.
- It's believed these beetles symbolize good things like strength, creativity, hard work, persistence, cooperation, and progress. If you find one and it crawls on you, you're lucky.
- The dogbane beetle belongs to one of the largest insect families in the world, with over 35,000 species.
- The dogbane beetle does not harm farming fields.

Praying Mantis

When this insect folds its front legs, it looks just like its praying. The Greek word *"mante"* means prophet. So, that means "praying prophet." But could they be praying before their meal? The praying mantis is not a picky eater. It is a predator and a beneficial insect that eats garden pests. It eats almost any insect it can catch with its raptorial (prey-catching) forelegs, like flies, moths, butterflies, caterpillars, and even frogs and fast-flying hummingbirds! In fact, female praying mantises are not very lovey-dovey. They may even eat their own mates! Oh, yikes! They really are not picky eaters. A most curious behavior!

Fun Facts

- In some cultures, seeing a praying mantis can be a sign of good luck or fortune.
- There are more than 2,000 different-looking species of praying mantises all over the world.
- The female praying mantis is much bigger than the male.
- Praying mantises don't bother people.

THIS IS A bizarre and strange-looking caterpillar. It has a bright-green saddle-shaped design on its back. It's confusing looking and appears to have a head on both ends of its body.

This caterpillar isn't friendly, and you mustn't EVER touch or nudge it. If you did, it hurts so much, you might cry like a baby and may need a doctor's care.

Its pokey little spines are like tiny, dangerous needles. They're attached to venom glands in this caterpillar's body. It's painful by just touching it!

Then this caterpillar will spin a silk cocoon (that may have stinging spines woven into it), rest inside, and transform (PUPATE). When the time is just right (up to 21 days), it comes out as a harmless adult brown fuzzy moth.

Fun (& Important!) Facts

- Always remember the rule: Insects with bright colors are always a warning sign. They either harm you or are poisonous if eaten by predators.
- Moths emerge from cocoons (soft case), and butterflies emerge from a chrysalis (hard case).
- The word *caterpillar* comes from the Old French word *"chatepelose"* which means hairy cat!
- Not all hairy caterpillars sting. But to be safe, it's best to leave them alone.

Leaf Cutter Bees

THIS IS A different kind of bee. It does not live in a hive with thousands of other bees. It is solitary (alone) with no hive at all. Instead, when the female is ready to lay her eggs, she looks for something hollow like a tree branch. Then she cuts neat little pieces of leaves with her MANDIBLES (claw-like scissors on the outside of her mouth) and places the leaf pieces into a hollow branch. Then mother bee visits flowers to collect pollen, which sticks to her furry underside, and nectar she eats and will spit up later to make a special food. She places the food on each little leaf piece and lays her eggs on top of the food. Then mother bee carefully wraps the leaf pieces up in a bundle. Baby bee inside will have nutritious food when it hatches.

Fun Facts

- Farmers love these bees because they POLLINATE (fertilize) crops and are gentle natured bees
- Native American folklore believed all insects are sacred beings who came before mankind.

Lady Beetle (Lady Bug)

THERE'S A STORY about how this beetle got its name. About 500 years ago, the farmers in Europe had problems with bugs eating their farming fields. They would pray to the Virgin Mary, also called "Our Lady," to protect their crops from destructive bugs. When they saw the black-and-red dotted beetles had come to their farms, they were happy. They noticed the beetles were eating the bugs that destroyed their fruits and vegetables. The farmers were thankful and believed the Virgin Mary had answered their prayers by sending these good bugs. And so, they named these good bugs "Beetle of Our Lady" or "Lady Beetle."

Fun Facts

- There are male and female lady beetles.
- Lady beetles are red with black dots. Their red color is a warning sign to other animals that they are yukky if eaten.
- All beetles have a harder shell around their body to protect their softer wings that are tucked and folded underneath, like a little protective armor.

IF YOU SEE a twinkle of little lights at night in the forest and woods, they could be fairies, but they're probably fireflies! These mystical and alluring insects talk to each other and find a mate with light from their tails. The firefly has chemicals in its tail that glow. It's called "cold light" because it's energy produced without heat! Firefly eggs and LARVAE (an insect's worm-like stage) glow too. Medicine and science are using these same chemicals in a firefly's tail to study human diseases as well as on spacecraft to detect life in outer space.

Fun Facts

- Summertime in Japan means firefly festivals. Legends say these insects symbolize love and are the souls of departed loved ones and the spirits of dead warriors.
- Fireflies have been around for over 100 million years!
- Fireflies are beetles, not flies.
- Fireflies are also known as lightning bugs.

Some Bug Words

Camouflage	ways animals blend in with their surroundings to protect themselves.
Chrysalis	a hard case spun by a caterpillar where it will rest inside and transform (pupate) before becoming an adult butterfly.
Cocoon	a silky case spun by a caterpillar where it will rest inside and transform (pupate) before becoming an adult moth.
Fossils	the impression of a prehistoric (before written history) form of life.
Larvae - (laar - vuh)	an insect's worm-like stage that hatches from an egg and looks very different from its parents.
Nectar	a sweet juice made by flowers to attract insects and birds.
Pollinate	the way plants get fertilized so they can reproduce. Which is often done by wind, by rain, and by insects, crawling and carrying the pollen on their legs when trying to get nectar from the sweet smell of flowers.
Pupa	the life stage of some insects that will transform into a completely different form, as an adult.

Insects Have a Place in Some Famous Quotes and Sayings

"Don't waste your time chasing butterflies.
Mend your garden, and the butterflies will come."
–Mario Quintana, Brazilian writer, born 1906

The greatest boxer who ever lived was Muhammad Ali.
He once said he "floats like a butterfly and stings like a bee"
to describe his own style of grace and power in the boxing ring.
–Muhammad Ali, Born in Louisville, Kentucky, 1942

"Love is like a butterfly, a rare and gentle thing"
–Dolly Parton, Born in Locust Ridge, Tennessee, 1946

"A girl should be like a butterfly. Pretty to see, hard to catch."
–Unknown

"It's not summer until the crickets sing."
–Greek saying

"When spiders unite, they can tie down a lion."
–Ethiopian saying

Would you like to invite butterflies to visit your garden? Here's what to do:

- Find out what butterflies are native where you live.

- Caterpillars eat the LEAVES of certain plants, and butterflies eat the NECTAR of certain native flowers.

- So, you'll need a plant the caterpillar likes to eat (the host plant). For example: the gulf fritillary caterpillar eats the leaves of the passion vine plant. Don't worry if the caterpillars have nibbled all the leaves on the passion vine. The leaves will come back the following year, and so will the butterflies. And you will also need plants that butterflies like to eat (the nectar plant). For example: the gulf fritillary butterfly drinks the nectar of native lantana flowers and other flowers too.

- Once you find the right plants for the caterpillars and butterflies in your yard, take care of your plants. Water them, watch them grow, be patient.

- And the BUTTERFLIES will come. In North Florida, the gulf fritillaries come September through November.

Acknowledgements

A BIG THANK YOU to Julie McConnell, who was graciously willing to share her knowledge and enthusiasm of the insect world towards this book. Julie is an entomologist and has been a Horticulture Extension Agent with the University of Florida IFAS Extension for many years in Bay County, FL. She is now the Washington County, FL. Horticulture Agent, and Northwest District (RSA). Julie creates and brings educational research-based classes to the public on vegetable gardening, fruiting trees, herbs, cooking, and more.

www.ingramcontent.com/pod-product-compliance
Lightning Source LLC
LaVergne TN
LVRC080725070526
838199LV00042B/739